THE BEER JOKE HANDBOOK

Brew HA HA

Hops Malone

Under The Leaves Publishing

To my incredible fans:

"The Beer Joke Handbook" is a frothy blend of humor and hops, crafted with you in mind. Your unwavering support and enthusiasm have fueled this journey. With each pun and punchline, I envisioned your smiles and heard your laughter.

This book is a toast to our shared love for comedy and brews, a tribute to the joy we find in life's lighter moments. May it bring you countless laughs and remind you of the camaraderie that laughter fosters.

With overflowing appreciation,

~ Hops Malone

Disclaimer: "The Beer Joke Handbook" is here to tickle your funny bone, not to challenge your liver. Remember, it's all about the laughs, not the lagers! Please, no beer chugging contests while reading. Always enjoy your brewskis responsibly, and if you laugh so hard you spill your drink, well, that's on us! Cheers to comedy, not inebriety!

Ale yeah!

3 RULES BEFORE WE GET STARTED:

Rule 1: Crack open a cold one and have backups ready.

Rule 2: Spread the joy! Read aloud your favorite jokes to friends and family.

Rule 3: Laughter Is Mandatory - If you don't laugh, you might need to check your pulse. It's all about having a hoppy time!

..relax, it's just a joke book

Round 1

~ Cheers

1 Yo mama so stupid, she tried to grow a beer garden.

Relax folks, we're just getting started ~ Hops Malone

2 What's the difference between this beer and your opinion? I asked for the beer.

3 Trust me, you can dance – Beer

ness
4 IPA lot when I drink beer, do you?

"Beer: Because no great story ever started with someone eating a salad."

5

A gorilla walks into a bar.

The gorilla sits down, grunts softly and points to a picture of a beer on the menu. The bartender pours the beer, hands it to the gorilla, who again grunts softly and nods.

The gorilla slaps a $100 bill down on the counter and slides it toward the bartender.

The bartender, figuring the gorilla was trained to do this, but would not be smart enough to count, takes the $100 and passes $10 back to the gorilla, who grunts and huffs in reply.

The gorilla downs the rest of the pint, turns to leave, and the bartender says out loud, to no one in particular, "Jeez, we don't get many gorillas in here."

The gorilla pauses, turns to stare at the bartender and gruffly says, "At $90 a beer, I'm not surprised."

6

I don't always drink beer, but when I do, I prefer to have five more!

7

Spilling a beer is the adult equivalent of losing a balloon.

8 Wife: "Honey, you need to cut back on beer; it's affecting your memory."
Husband: "Nonsense! I never forget to buy more beer!"

9 Give a man a beer, he wastes a hour. Teach a man to brew, he wastes a lifetime.

10

Wife: "I don't understand why you love beer so much."
Husband: "Well, it's like a perfect marriage. It's always there for me, and it never talks back!"

"Beer: The cause of and solution to all of life's problems."

THE BEER JOKE HANDBOOK

11 A horse walks into a bar and orders a beer. The bartender asks, "Why the long face?" The horse replies, "I just realized I'm in the wrong joke. I was supposed to walk into a stable!"

12 If at first you don't succeed, it's not a twist-top... use a bottle opener.

13 What's a beer's favorite type of humor? Wit-ty jokes!

14 I drink beer because I'm too lazy to walk
They say you should walk 10000 steps, the AA only requires 12.

15

Did you know that beer makes you lean? On walls, toilets and friends.

16

Wife: "They say wine improves with age." Husband: "Beer doesn't need to age; it's already perfect!"

17 What did the beer say to the glass? "You're the reason I'm half empty!"

18 I have a beer drinking problem – my fridge is too small to hold all the craft beers I want to try!

19 What kind of beer does a vampire drink? Bloodweiser.

20

A duck waddles into a bar and says to the bartender, "Do you have any grapes?"

The bartender replies, "Sorry, we don't have grapes. This is a bar, we serve beer."

The next day, the duck returns and asks, "Do you have any grapes?"

The bartender says, "I told you yesterday, we don't have grapes! And if you ask again, I'll nail your beak to the bar!"

The following day, the duck walks in and asks, "Do you have any nails?"

The bartender confusedly says, "No, we don't have any nails."

The duck smiles and asks, "Do you have any grapes?"

21

Why did the drunk woman bring a ladder to the bar? She heard the drinks were on the house!

22

Why did the beer get a job as a detective? It wanted to crack open cold cases!

"In a world full of choices, I'll choose beer."

23
Why did the beer file a police report? It got mugged!

24
How do you know if someone really likes craft beer? Don't worry they will tell you.

25 My beer drinking problem is that I can't decide which brewery to visit next!

26 I don't trust stairs when I've had too much beer? They're always up to something!

27
Why don't skeletons drink beer? They don't have the stomach for it!

28
What is a Pirates favorite beer?
P B Rrrrrrrrrrrrrr

29 Why don't scientists trust atoms when they go out drinking? Because they make up everything, just like my drunk friends!

30 What's the difference between a drunk person and a glass of beer? The glass of beer doesn't talk trash after a few rounds!

"You can't buy happiness, but you can buy beer, and that's kind of the same thing."

31 A guy walks into a bar and asks the bartender for a beer and a double entendre. The bartender gives it to him.

32 How do you know when you've had too much beer? When you start hugging the toilet bowl and saying, "I love you, man!"

33 What's a beer's favorite type of music? Hop-hop!

34 I've got a beer drinking problem – my friends keep drinking all my beer!

35
Husband: "Cheers to us, my love!"
Wife: "Cheers to you remembering our anniversary this time!"

36
Why did the beer go to therapy? It had a drinking problem!

37 My man cave has an open door policy. Bring the beer, and I'll open the door.

38 Beauty is in the eye of the beer holder.

THE BEER JOKE HANDBOOK

39 What did the beer say to the wine after a night out? "You're grape, but I'm barley hanging on!"

40 A guy walked into a bar carrying a slab of asphalt. He said to the bartender, "I'll take a beer, and one for the road!"

You make my heart malt

41 Why did the scarecrow win an award? Because he was outstanding in his field... with a cold beer!

42 My doctor said I should watch my drinking. So now I drink in front of a mirror. Problem solved!

43

Wife: "Wine is so refined."
Husband: "Beer is so refreshingly unpretentious!"

44

A guy walked into a bar with a duck on his head. The bartender looked puzzled and asked, "What's with the duck?" The duck replied, "I'm just here to keep an eye on my bill!"

"Beer: It's not just a beverage; it's a lifestyle."

45 How do you balance beer intake? With a beer in each hand, of course!

46 Stop trying to make everyone happy. You're not beer.

47 Why did the beer go to the gym? It wanted a six-pack!

48

A guy walked into a bar and ordered a beer with jumper cables wrapped around his neck. The bartender looked at him and said, "You can stay, but don't try to start anything!"

49 What kind of beer do ants drink?
Bug lite.

50 A guy walked into a bar and asked the bartender for a beer. The bartender asked, "Are you over 21?" The guy replied, "Of course, I'm barley legal!"

Beer...because you can't drink bacon

INTERMISSION

Think of this as a beer break for your laughter.

Don't worry

There are plenty more jokes on tap

Round 2

Pace Yourself

~ Cheers

51

An iceberg walks into a bar. Orders a single beer and leaves $100.
Bartender: Wow! That's way too generous!
Iceberg: That's just the tip of the iceberg!

52

A guy walked into a bar and ordered a beer. The bartender said, "Sorry, we're all out." The guy looked surprised and said, "That's un-beer-lievable!"

53

I told my buddy I would stop drinking beer for a month.

He said, "That's great! I'll see you on February 31st."

54

Why is a beer drinker better than a wine drinker? Because beer drinkers never whine about their beverage choices!

55 A neutron walks into a bar and asks, "How much for a beer?" The bartender replies, "For you, no charge!"

56 Beer drinkers have better balance than wine drinkers. They can walk a straight line after a few pints, while wine drinkers stumble and blame it on their terroir!

57

Beer drinkers can handle a keg stand, while wine drinkers struggle to pour a glass without spilling.

58

A skeleton walks into a bar. Orders a beer and a mop.

"Friends don't let friends drink bad beer."

59

What do you call a beer in the freezer?
Polar beer.

60

Got home to find my wife had left a note on the fridge that said, "This isn't working I'm going to my mother's"
I opened up the fridge.
The light was on and the beer was cold.
...I'm not sure what she was talking about.

61 Beer drinkers are always ready for a game of beer pong. Wine drinkers are too busy sniffing their glasses to compete!

62 How does a man plan for the future? He buys two cases of beer.

63 Steps for starting a success beer business.

Step 1: Start a beer company named Responsibly.

Step 2: Watch every beer company promote your beer for free at the end of their commercials.

Step 3: Enjoy your mansion

"I'm on a beer-only diet. I lost three days last week."

64 Wife: "Do you remember our wedding day like it was yesterday?"
Husband: "Oh, definitely! It was the happiest day of my life – until I discovered IPA!"

65 What do you never say to a policeman?
"Sure, let me grab my license. Can you hold my beer?"

66

Roses are red, violets are blue. Poems are hard. Beer!

67

An SEO professional walks into a bar, pub, inn, tavern, cafe, beer parlor and orders a beer.

"Beer: Proof that God loves us and wants us to be happy."

68

A guy walks into a bar and orders a fruit punch. The bartender says, "Pal, we serve beer here. If you want punch, you'll have to stand in that line." The guy looks around, but there is no punchline...

THE BEER JOKE HANDBOOK

69 Beer is made from hops.
Hops is a plant.
Beer = salad!

70 Riddle: What kind of bird
and how much beer does it
take to get it drunk?

Toucans.

71 This beer tastes like I'm not going to work in the morning.

72 Husband: "I heard that drinking beer makes you smarter."
Wife: "Oh, really? So why don't you have another one and let's test that theory!"

73 Beer makes you smarter. Well…it made Budweiser.

74 I gave my dog a beer last night. I asked him how he felt this morning. He said ruff.

75 Mike: "A Moose walks into a bar and orders a beer."

Tom: "Wow, really a Moose???"
Mike: " ...Nah, I'm just drunk"

76 The earth is rotating at over 1000 miles an hour. However, humans don't feel the effect of it until the 9th or 10th beer.

THE BEER JOKE HANDBOOK

77 My buddy asked me if I'd ever tried a slice of orange in my beer.
I told him "Once in a Blue Moon".

78 You shouldn't drink beer every day. That's why I only drink at night.

79 Roses are red, violets are blue, forget the wine, beer pairs better with you.

80 Husband: "Beer is like a hug in a mug!"
Wife: "Well, if you love it so much, why don't you marry it?"
Husband: ".... Is that even possible?"

81

A penguin walks into a bar, waddles up to the counter, and asks the bartender, "I'll have a beer and have you seen my brother?" The bartender replies, "I don't know, what does he look like?"

"Beer: Helping people forget their differences and bond over a common love."

82 A sandwich walks into a bar and orders a beer. The bartender says, "Sorry, we don't serve food here"

83 What's an insect's favorite beer?
Gnatty.

84

A Roman walks into a bar, holds up two fingers, and says..
Five Beers, please!

85

Somebody should make a beer called "Occasionally". So when asked, I can say, "I only drink occasionally".

86
What's a beer's favorite TV show? "Hoppy Days"!

87
Husband: "I'm feeling adventurous tonight. I'll try the strongest beer they have!"
Wife: "And I'm feeling responsible tonight. I'll drive us home!"

88 What do you call a fish that drinks too much beer? A beer-a-cuda!

89 Did you hear about the guy who spilled his beer while riding a dolphin? He says he spilled his beer on porpoise.

90

A guy walks into a bar and sees a sign that says, "Free Beer for Life! Just ask the bartender." The guy excitedly asks the bartender, "Is that true?" The bartender replies, "Nope.."

"Beer: It's not just a beverage; it's a lifestyle."

THE BEER JOKE HANDBOOK

91 What's the difference between beer nuts and deer nuts? Beer nuts cost about a dollar fifty while deers nuts are under a buck.

92 I don't always drink beer, but when I do, my friends have to carry me home!

93

I drank so much beer that I woke up this morning with a note from my liver saying, "We need to talk."

94

A guy walks into a bar with a steering wheel sticking out of his pants and orders a beer. The bartender asks, "Hey, what's with the steering wheel?" The guy replies, "I don't know, but it's driving me nuts!"

"Beer: The answer you were looking for, even if you didn't know you were asking the question."

95 I don't have a beer drinking problem. I drink. I get drunk. I fall down. No problem!

96 I told my wife I quit drinking, but she doesn't believe me. I guess actions speak louder when they're stumbling!

97 A guy walks into a bar and orders a beer. He gulps it down, looks into his wallet, and asks the bartender for another. The bartender asks, "Is something bothering you?" The guy replies, "My doctor says I have to drink plenty of liquids.

98 Never look at your beer as half empty. Look at it as halfway to your next beer.

99 Wife: "You know, there's a beer out there that perfectly describes you."
Husband: "Oh really? What's it called?"
Wife: "Domestic!"

100 How do you know you've reached your beer limit? When you realize you can't remember any of the beer jokes you just read!

HOPS MALONE

You should be feeling a strong sense of pride right now ~ Hops Malone

ABOUT THE AUTHOR

Hops Malone

Hops Malone, the brilliant mind behind "The Beer Joke Handbook - Brew Ha Ha," was born with a twinkle in his eye and a frothy head full of ideas. Legend has it that his first words were not "mama" or "dada," but rather "ale" and "pilsner." From an early age, he displayed an uncanny ability to turn everyday situations into uproarious punchlines, much to the delight of his family and friends.

Today, Hops Malone continues to tour breweries and comedy clubs, bringing his unique blend of wit and hops to audiences far and wide. With his book, he invites readers to join him on a laughter-filled journey where each joke is crafted as carefully as a master brewer perfecting their recipe. So raise your glass to Hops Malone – the man who turned jokes into an art as refreshing as a cold beer on a hot day!

WHAT HOPS MALONE
FANS ARE SAYING

"Hops Malone's jokes flow as smoothly as a perfectly poured pint."

"I like beer & I like Hops!

"Laughter on tap – Hops Malone's comedy is a refreshing delight!"

"Brewing brilliance meets belly laughs"

"Hops Malone is the master of hops and hilarity – a perfect pairing!"

"I love laughing and I love beer - Thanks Hops!

"Hops Malone's jokes are like a fine aged ale – and I drink anything!

"Raise your glass to Hops Malone – his jokes are the life of the party!"

"In a world of stand-up, Hops Malone's humor stands out"

MEDIA REVIEWS:

"Hops Malone's 'The Beer Joke Handbook' is a frothy concoction of wit and humor that pairs perfectly with any pint. Prepare to be both enlightened and entertained while sipping on these hearty laughs."

- A. Quenchwell, Brews & Chuckles Mag

In 'Brew Ha Ha,' Hops Malone delivers a refreshing blend of clever wordplay and hoppy punchlines. This book is a must-read for both beer enthusiasts and joke lovers alike."

- Oliver Witstein, Pint&Puns.org

"Hops Malone taps into the perfect formula for laughter. Each joke is crafted with the precision of a master brewer, resulting in a book that's as satisfying as a cold pint on a hot day."

- Samuel Whitbier, Laugh Brews Weekly 'LBW'

"Hops Malone's humor is like a crisp lager – it goes down smooth and leaves a smile on your face. Cheers to you Hops!

- Ale Witton, Jokes & Pours Gazette

WANT TO SUPPORT HOPS MALONE?

Hops is a man of pride. He takes his work seriously & one pint at a time.

Please consider leaving a **5 Star Review on Amazon**. This is one of the best things you can do for the author.

Simple how-to guide:
1. Go to: Amazon.com
2. Search for: "The Beer Joke Handbook"
3. Click on: "The Beer Joke Handbook"
4. Click on: "Write a customer review"
5. Type: "Best thing ever! 5 stars"
6. "Submit"

Cheers ~ Hops Malone

Printed in Great Britain
by Amazon